Other Helen Exley Giftbooks:

Cat Quotations	Teddy Bear Quotations
Golf Quotations	Music Lover's Quotations
Book Lover's Quotations	Horse Quotations
Garden Lover's Quotations	Love Quotations
Friendship Quotations	Cricket Quotations

Published in the USA in 1992 by Exley Giftbooks
Published in Great Britain in 1992 by Exley Publications Ltd

12 11 10 9 8

Series editor Helen Exley
The moral right of the author has been asserted.

ISBN 1-85015-318-3

A copy of the CIP data is available from the British Library on request.

Edited by Helen Exley
Pictures researched by Image Select International.
Typeset by Delta, Watford.
Printed in China.

**Exley Publications Ltd, 16 Chalk Hill, Watford,
Herts WD1 4BN, United Kingdom
Exley Publications LLC, 232 Madison Avenue, Suite 1206,
NY 10016, USA**

Exley Publications is very grateful to the following individuals and organizations for permission to reproduce their pictures: Archiv Für Kunst, Berlin; Atkinson Art Gallery, Southport; Bradford City Art Gallery; Bridgeman Art Library; Bury Art Gallery; Christie's, London; Fine Art Society, London; Giraudon, Paris; Gavin Graham Gallery, London; Magyar Nemzeti Gallery, Budapest; Musée des Beaux-Arts, Quimper; Musée Carnavalet, Paris; Nasjonalgalleriet, Oslo; Oldham Art Gallery, Lancs; Scala; Julian Simon Fine Art, London; Spink & Son Ltd, London; Towneley Hall Art Gallery, Burnley; Turku Art Museum, Finland; Waterhouse & Dodd, London; Whitford & Hughes, London; Christopher Wood Art Gallery, London.

HAPPINESS QUOTATIONS

A COLLECTION OF THOUGHTFUL WORDS AND BEAUTIFUL PAINTINGS

– ◆ –

A Helen Exley Giftbook

EXLEY

NEW YORK • WATFORD, UK

"Nothing is worth more than this day."

JOHANN WOLFGANG VON GOETHE (1749-1832)

"Yesterday is a cancelled cheque; tomorrow is a promissory note; today is the only cash you have - so spend it wisely."

KAY LYONS

"The sense of existence is the greatest happiness."

BENJAMIN DISRAELI (1804-1881)

"And only when we are no longer afraid do we begin to live in every experience, painful or joyous; to live in gratitude for every moment, to live abundantly."

DOROTHY THOMPSON (1894-1961)

"Write it on your heart that every day is the best day in the year."

RALPH WALDO EMERSON (1803-1882)

"...the little hills rejoice on every side. The pastures are clothed with flocks; the valleys also are covered over with corn; they shout for joy, they also sing."

PSALMS 65:12 AND 13

"Earth's crammed with heaven."

ELIZABETH BARRETT BROWNING (1806-1861)

"Today a new sun rises for me; everything lives, everything is animated, everything seems to speak to me of my passion, everything invites me to cherish it..."

ANNE DE LENCLOS (1616-1706)

LOVE

"Love and joy are twins, or born
of each other."

WILLIAM HAZLITT (1778-1830)

"The cure for all the ills and wrongs, the
cares, the sorrows, and the crimes of
humanity, all lie in the one word 'love'. It is
the divine vitality that everywhere produces
and restores life."

LYDIA MARIA CHILD (1802-1880)

"The moment you have in your heart this
extra-ordinary thing called love and feel the
depth, the delight, the ecstasy of it, you will
discover that for you the world
is transformed."

J. KRISHNAMURTI (1895-1986)

"There is only one way to happiness and that is to cease worrying about things which are beyond the power of our will."

EPICTETUS (1st century AD)

"Life is like a blanket too short. You pull it up and your toes rebel, you yank it down and shivers meander about your shoulder; but cheerful folks manage to draw their knees up and pass a very comfortable night."

MARION HOWARD

"My life has no purpose, no direction, no aim, no meaning, and yet I'm happy. I can't figure it out. What am I doing right?"

CHARLES M. SCHULZ, b.1922

ENJOY IT!

If your nose is close to the grindstone
And you hold it there long enough
In time you'll say there's no such thing
As brooks that babble and birds that sing
These three will all your world compose
Just you, the stone and your poor old nose.

On a two hundred-year-old stone in a country cemetery

"...Life, for all its agonies of despair and loss
and guilt, is exciting and beautiful, amusing
and artful and endearing, full of liking and
love, at times a poem and a high adventure,
at times noble and at times very gay; and
whatever (if anything) is to come after it
- we shall not have this life again."

ROSE MACAULAY (1881-1958)

"Happiness is in the comfortable
companionship of friends."

PAM BROWN, b.1928

"Grief can take care of itself, but to get the full
value of a joy you must have somebody to
divide it with."

MARK TWAIN (1835-1910)

"True happiness is of a retired nature and
an enemy to pomp and noise; it arises, in
the first place, from the enjoyment of
one's self; and, in the next, from the
friendship and conversations of a few
select companions."

JOSEPH ADDISON (1672-1719)

Pleasure, or wrong or rightly understood,
Our greatest evil, or our greatest good.

ALEXANDER POPE (1688-1744)

"So long as man is alive and free, he will, in
one way or another, seek that which gives him
pleasure. But to seek is not necessarily to
find...The basis of happiness is abundance of
life, and abundance of life is a real thing..."

DAVID STARR JORDAN

SURPRISED BY JOY

"The moments of happiness we enjoy
take us by surprise.
It is not that we seize them, but that
they seize us."

ASHLEY MONTAGU, b.1905

"There is no such thing as the pursuit
of happiness, but there is the
discovery of joy."

JOYCE GRENFELL (1910-1980)

"I don't think that...one gets a flash of
happiness once, and never again; it is there
within you, and it will come as certainly
as death..."

ISAK DINESEN (BARONESS KAREN BLIXEN) (1885-1962)

"Happiness is rarely a reward.
More often a totally unexpected gift."

PAM BROWN, b.1928

"Happiness sneaks in through a door you
didn't know you left open."

JOHN BARRYMORE (1882-1942)

"If you want to be happy, be."

LEO TOLSTOY (1828-1910)

"To fill the hour - that is happiness; to fill the hour, and leave no crevice for a repentance or an approval."

RALPH WALDO EMERSON (1803-1882)

SHARING HAPPINESS

"Happiness is a perfume you cannot pour on
others without getting a few drops
on yourself."

UNKNOWN

"There is a wonderful, mystical law of nature
that the three things we crave most in life -
happiness, freedom, and peace of mind -
are always attained by giving them
to someone else."

UNKNOWN

All who joy would win
Must share it - happiness was born a twin.

LORD BYRON (1788-1824)

"Happiness itself is sufficient excuse. Beautiful things are right and true; so beautiful actions are those pleasing to the gods. Wise people have an inward sense of what is beautiful, and the highest wisdom is to trust this intuition and be guided by it. The answer to the last appeal of what is right lies within a person's own breast. Trust thyself."

ARISTOTLE (384-322 BC)

"If I were to choose the sights, the sounds, the fragrances I most would want to see and hear and smell - among all the delights of the open world - on a final day on earth, I think I would choose these: the clear, ethereal song of a white-throated sparrow singing at dawn; the smell of pine trees in the heat of noon; the lonely calling of Canada geese; the sight of a dragon-fly glinting in the sunshine; the voice of a hermit thrush far in a darkening wood at evening; and - most spiritual and moving of sights - the white cathedral of a cumulus cloud floating serenely in the blue of the sky."

EDWIN WAY TEALE

— ◆ —

ANOTHER DOOR OPENS

"When one door of happiness closes, another opens; but often we look so long at the closed door that we do not see the one which has been opened for us."

HELEN KELLER (1880-1968)

"We can easily manage, if we will only take each day, the burden appointed for it. But the load will be too heavy for us if we carry yesterday's burden over again today, and then add the burden of the morrow to the weight before we are required to bear it."

JOHN NEWTON (1725-1807)

"Talk happiness. The world is sad enough. Without your woe. No path is wholly rough."

ELLA WHEELER WILCOX (1850-1919)

SOLITUDE

"I find it wholesome to be alone the greater part of the time. To be in company, even with the best, is soon wearisome and dissipating. I love to be alone. I never found the companion that was so companionable as solitude. We are for the most part more lonely when we go abroad among men than when we stay in our chambers. A man thinking or working is always alone, let him be where he will. Solitude is not measured by the miles of space that intervene between a man and his fellows. The really diligent student in one of the crowded hives of Cambridge College is as solitary as a dervish in the desert."

HENRY DAVID THOREAU (1817-1862)

"One is happy as a result of one's own efforts, once one knows the necessary ingredients of happiness - simple tastes, a certain degree of courage, self-denial to a point, love of work, and above all, a clear conscience.
Happiness is no vague dream, of that I now feel certain."

GEORGE SAND (AMANDINE AURORE LUCIE DUPIN) (1804-1876)

— ◆ —

"The way I see it, if you want the rainbow,
you gotta put up with the rain."

DOLLY PARTON, b.1946

"Our greatest glory is not in never falling, but
in rising every time we fall."

CONFUCIUS (551-479 BC)

IN TIMES OF TROUBLE

"When you get into a tight place and everything goes against you, till it seems as though you could not hang on a minute longer, never give up then, for that is just the place and time that the tide will turn."

HARRIET BEECHER STOWE (1811-1896)

"If I were asked to give what I consider the single most useful bit of advice for all humanity it would be this: Expect trouble as an inevitable part of life and when it comes, hold your head high, look it squarely in the eye and say, 'I will be bigger than you. You cannot defeat me.'"

ANN LANDERS, b.1918

BELIEVE IT!

"Believe that life is worth living and your
belief will help create the fact."

WILLIAM JAMES (1842-1910)

"Far away there in the sunshine are my
highest aspirations. I may not reach them, but
I can look up and see their beauty, believe in
them, and try to follow where they lead."

LOUISA MAY ALCOTT (1832-1888)

"The great successful people of the world ...
think ahead and create their mental picture,
and then go to work materializing that picture
in all its details, filling in here, adding a little
there, altering this a bit and that a bit, but
steadily building - steadily building."

ROBERT COLLIER

"Money never prevented anybody from being happy or unhappy."

EDDIE BARCLAY

"The question of wealth is like chasing a rainbow. I have hunted a rainbow in an aeroplane, but always in the end it was just grey mist. It seems to me that the pursuit of riches is such an exacting task that he who strives for them must soon forget what it was he originally hoped to acquire. Even if he remembers, he is so old, and so weary, or both, that the star he strove to reach turns out to be merely mist, grey mist, and nothing more. What we thought was happiness is so seldom what we thought it was."

THEO STEPHENS,
from *"My Garden's Good-Night"*

"Joy is not in things; it is in us."

RICHARD WAGNER (1813-1883)

"It is in the enjoyment and not in mere
possession that makes for happiness."

MICHEL DE MONTAIGNE (1533-1592)

FOR A PURPOSE

"We act as though comfort and luxury were the chief requirements of life, when all that we need to make us really happy is something to be enthusiastic about."

CHARLES KINGSLEY (1819-1875)

"If a man has important work, and enough leisure and income to enable him to do it properly, he is in possession of as much happiness as is good for any of the children of Adam."

R. H. TAWNEY (1880-1962)

"Existence is a strange bargain. Life owes us little; we owe it everything. The only true happiness comes from squandering ourselves for a purpose."

WILLIAM COWPER (1731-1800)

SIMPLICITY

"To be without some of the things you want is an indispensable part of happiness."

BERTRAND RUSSELL (1872-1970)

"He knew how to be poor without the least hint of squalor or inelegance...He chose to be rich by making his wants few."

RALPH WALDO EMERSON (1803-1882),
about Henry David Thoreau

"Grant to me that I may be made beautiful in my soul within, and that all external possessions be in harmony with my inner man. May I consider the wise man rich, and may I have such wealth as only the self-restrained man can bear or endure."

PRAYER OF SOCRATES

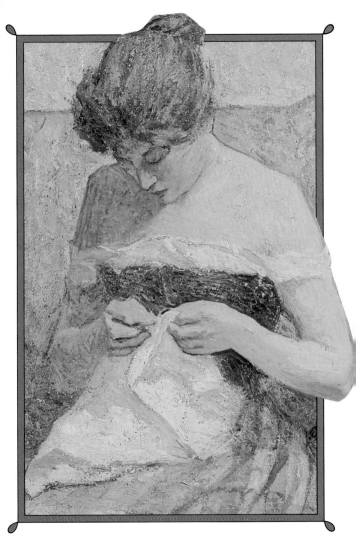

"We have no more right to consume happiness without producing it than to consume wealth without producing it."

GEORGE BERNARD SHAW (1856-1950)

"In the pursuit of happiness half the world is on the wrong scent. They think it consists in having and getting, and in being served by others. Happiness is really found in giving and in serving others."

HENRY DRUMMOND (1851-1897)

"The longer I live the more I am convinced that the one thing worth living for and dying for is the privilege of making someone more happy and more useful. No man who ever does anything to lift his fellows ever makes a sacrifice."

BOOKER T. WASHINGTON (1856-1915)

"Treasure the love you receive above all. It will survive long after your gold and good health have vanished."

OG MANDINO

— ◆ —

What is this life if, full of care,
We have no time to stand and stare?

No time to stand beneath the boughs
And stare as long as sheep or cows.

No time to see, when woods we pass,
Where squirrels hide their nuts in grass.

No time to see, in broad daylight,
Streams full of stars, like skies at night.

No time to turn at Beauty's glance,
And watch her feet, how they can dance.

No time to wait till her mouth can
Enrich that smile her eyes began.

A poor life this if, full of care,
We have no time to stand and stare.

W. H. DAVIES (1871-1940)

– ◆ –

DON'T WASTE IT!

"There is no duty we so much underrate as
the duty of being happy."

ROBERT LOUIS STEVENSON (1850-1894)

"Why not seize the pleasure at once? How
often is happiness destroyed by preparation,
foolish preparation!"

JANE AUSTEN (1775-1817)

"The most wasted day of all is that on which
we have not laughed."

SEBASTIEN R. N. CHAMFORT (1741-1794)

Throw your heart out in front of you.
And run ahead to catch it.

ARAB PROVERB

AS A BUTTERFLY

"Happiness is as a butterfly, which, when
pursued, is always just beyond our grasp,
but which, if you will sit down quietly,
may alight upon you."

NATHANIEL HAWTHORNE (1804-1864)

"Pleasure is frail like a dewdrop, while it
laughs it dies."

SIR RABINDRANATH TAGORE (1861-1941)

He who bends to himself a joy
Doth the wingéd life destroy;
But he who kisses a joy as it flies
Lives in Eternity's sunrise.

WILLIAM BLAKE (1757-1827)

"To be able to find joy in another's joy: that is the secret of happiness."

GEORGES BERNANOS (1888-1948)

— ◆ —

"The soul that perpetually overflows with kindness and sympathy will always be cheerful."

PARKE GODWIN

— ◆ —

"Is it so small a thing to have enjoyed the sun,
to have lived light in the spring,
to have loved, to have thought,
to have done?"

MATTHEW ARNOLD (1822-1888)

— ◆ —

CONTENTMENT

Contentment is the philosopher's stone,
which turns all it toucheth into gold;
the poor man is rich with it, the rich
man poor without it.

PROVERB

"If it be my lot to crawl, I will crawl
contentedly; if to fly, I will fly with alacrity;
but as long as I can possibly avoid it, I will
never be unhappy."

SYDNEY SMITH (1771-1845)

"Accept the pain, cherish the joys, resolve
the regrets; then can come the best of
benedictions - 'If I had my life to live
over, I'd do it all the same.'"

JOAN MCINTOSH